The Two Shall Be
ONE

Preparing Your Church Wedding

A Workbook for Engaged Couples

Revised in light of present marriage ritual

Kathleen McAnany
Peter Schavitz, C.SS.R.

LIGUORI
PUBLICATIONS

One Liguori Drive
Liguori, MO 63057-9999
(314) 464-2500

Imprimi Potest:
James Shea, C.SS.R.
Provincial, St. Louis Province
The Redemptorists

Imprimatur:
+ Edward J. O'Donnell, D.D.
Auxiliary Bishop, Archdiocese of St. Louis

ISBN 0-89243-676-X
Library of Congress Catalog Card Number: 94-77056

Cover and interior design by Christine Kraus
Cover photo courtesy of Dee Vaeth
Background photo: Image Masters

Contents

Work Sheets, Final Liturgy Sheets, and Music Planning Guides inserted between pages 40 and 41

Introduction

Congratulations! The two of you have made an important decision to enter the sacrament of matrimony. This booklet is intended to help you prepare the liturgy that will celebrate your sacrament. The ceremony you are planning should influence the rest of your day, the rest of your lives. While this booklet cannot cover all the specifics of local custom, it is structured to take you step by step through the common ingredients of a wedding.

In the Catholic tradition, a wedding can be celebrated by itself or in the context of a Mass. Between pages 40 and 41 are work sheets that will help you plan your wedding. One work sheet details the components of *a wedding within the context of a Mass;* the other details the components of *a wedding that is celebrated outside the context of a Mass.* Select the one you need, gently tug it loose from the center staples, discard the other, and record your choices as you work through this booklet. Neither work sheet follows the chronological order of the service. Rather, they begin with the Scripture readings you will select; the rest of your ceremony and choices flow from this selection.

On pages 68 to 76, you will find "Other Ceremonial Options" and "Further Celebration Considerations." You may want to read these sections before beginning your task; they address many of your concerns regarding music, the procession, flowers, candles, runners, photographers, flowers to Mary, and so on.

Also between pages 40 and 41, you will find the "Final Liturgy Sheets": one for *a wedding ceremony with a Mass,* and one for *a wedding ceremony without a Mass.* When you finish planning your ceremony using the appropriate work sheet, and decide on music with your musician, complete your "Final Liturgy Sheet" and give it to the person officiating at your wedding. These pages provide that person with a list of options you have chosen in the chronological order in which they happen during your ceremony.

"Music Planning Guides" are found between pages 40 and 41 as well; one is for *a wedding with a Mass,* and one is for *a wedding without a Mass.* To reduce the amount of time needed to work on wedding music, cut out the appropriate "Music Planning Guide" and bring it with you when you meet with your musician.

If you have questions as you go through this booklet, the person working with you on behalf of the parish community will help you.

Preliminary Considerations

Wedding Location

All kinds of memories surround the structures that served as your "homes" throughout your childhood. While the structures influenced your lives, however, it was the people—parents, siblings, neighbors, and extended family—that gave those structures life and meaning.

In the same way, your faith has been nurtured in a parish family, your brothers and sisters in Jesus. While the structure may not be the place of your dreams, it is where your faith was nurtured by those you grew up with as a Catholic.

Recognizing this, it is both customary and Church law to celebrate the sacrament of matrimony within the parish of either the bride or the groom, if both are Catholic. If only one is Catholic, the wedding is normally at the Catholic's parish. To celebrate your wedding in a Catholic church other than your own parish, you must secure the permission of the Catholic bride and/or groom's pastor and the permission of the pastor where you want the ceremony to take place.

It is permissible for a Catholic to marry in another Christian church. For such a wedding to be valid and recognized by the Catholic Church, proper dispensations must be obtained by the Catholic party from the Catholic's pastor.

Wedding Season, Time, and Date

When choosing a date for your wedding, be aware of the Church's liturgical calendar. For example, it is permissible to celebrate a wedding during Lent, but because it is a penitential season, Catholics are asked to avoid this season, which begins sometime in February and ends with Easter. Because of the austereness of the Lenten season, parishes purposely attempt to create a desert atmosphere of preparation for the great and joyous feast and season of Easter. The festive climate of a wedding can be a disruption to this atmosphere.

Many dioceses require notification of your intentions to marry four to six months prior to your wedding date. This gives both you and the people who will assist you in planning and preparing for your celebration time to address all concerns and details. This period also gives the two of you time to reflect further on the key ingredients of the matrimonial relationship you plan to embrace.

Before deciding on a wedding date, call the parish office as well to determine the availability of the church and ministers; many parishes have prearranged weekend time slots for weddings. Some parishes offer Friday evenings and Saturdays; some parishes also offer Sunday afternoons and evenings.

In setting the time of your wedding, consider your photography preferences. This may influence the time you'll need between the celebration at the church and the celebration at the reception.

If you are looking to cut expenses, you may want to consider a Saturday morning wedding followed by a simple reception or/luncheon in the church hall or reception place.

Wedding Ceremony

In the Catholic Church, a wedding can take place by itself or it can be celebrated in the context of a Mass. If both of you are Catholic, it's natural to celebrate your wedding during a Mass. If one of you is not Catholic, then your wedding should be outside of a Mass context. In some dioceses the bishop has made an exception for Catholics marrying a baptized non-Catholic for the wedding to take place within a Mass. Ask the minister officiating at your wedding what the diocesan policy is for weddings of Catholics to baptized non-Catholics and what would be best given your situation.

Rehearsal Time

When reserving the church, think ahead in terms of a rehearsal date and time. Take into consideration the people who will need to be at the rehearsal and the distances they must travel.

Prior to the rehearsal, contact the people coming and inform them about appropriate attire and conduct. Some people do not know that we, as Catholics, out of respect for the presence of Jesus in the Blessed Sacrament, do not smoke or drink in church.

Wedding Preparation and Programs

The goal of a marriage-preparation program is to help you better understand what it means to be a sacramental couple in the Catholic Church. Such programs focus on the key characteristics your present and future relationship should possess, and what your strengths and weaknesses may be as individuals and as a couple. There are three basic types of marriage-preparation programs.

Pre-Cana: This program is usually coordinated by the diocese and offered at local parishes. The program may be presented in a one- or two-day format and is attended by a large number of couples. Presentations are made on a number of key areas pertaining to the sacrament of matrimony. After each presentation, you are usually given time to privately discuss the topic further as it applies to your relationship.

Sponsor Couple Program: Some parishes train married couples to work with engaged couples who are planning to marry in the parish. Over a period of five or six weeks, you and maybe one or two other engaged couples will meet with a married couple to discuss the sacrament and how it is lived out daily.

Engaged Encounter Weekend: This weekend takes place at a retreat center or a similar facility. It begins Friday evening and concludes Sunday; couples are provided overnight accommodations in the facility. Several couples present the weekend, and a priest is there for at least a portion of the time. A married couple will make a presentation on some aspect of their matrimonial relationship and then give you time, individually and as a couple, to reflect on and discuss the topic further. This weekend is not available in every diocese.

Find out what programs are available in your diocese and decide which one best meets your needs. Discuss these options with the parish staff member working with you. In some cases, such as the Engaged Encounter weekend, registrations should be made far in advance of program dates.

The Readings

Instructions

It is up to you to determine the readings for your service. The readings you choose form the foundation for all your other choices.

Rather than plowing through all the possible readings at one sitting, read and reflect on each one, individually and as a couple. Each reading is followed by a set of questions that will guide your reflections. After listening to each other's reflections, ask yourselves what God may be saying to both of you about your relationship, about matrimony.

Take notes during your private and couple reflections. After you have reflected on all the readings, review your notes and choose the readings that speak most meaningfully to you about the sacrament of matrimony that you are entering. Your notes will also help you complete the section titled "Focusing on Your Choices."

You may select two or three Scripture readings. Should you decide to have two readings, the first reading may be from either the Old Testament or the New Testament; the second reading should be selected from the gospels. Should you choose to have three readings, the first reading is from the Old Testament (or the Acts of the Apostles during the season of Easter) and is followed by the responsorial psalm. (It is best to sing the responsorial psalm if you have a vocalist. Your musician can help you in this selection. In the absence of a vocalist, the responsorial psalm is read. It follows the first reading in all weddings.) The second reading should be selected from the New Testament, and the third reading is selected from the gospels.

Old Testament Readings

Old Testament Reading Number 101
(Genesis 1:26-28, 31)

A reading from the book of Genesis

God said: "Let us make man in our own image, after our likeness. Let them have dominion over the fish of the sea, the birds of the air, and the cattle, and over all the wild animals and all the creatures that crawl on the ground."

God created man in his image;
in the divine image he created him;
male and female he created them.

God blessed them, saying: "Be fertile and multiply; fill the earth and subdue it. Have dominion over the fish of the sea, the birds of the air, and all the living things that move on the earth."…God looked at everything he had made, and he found it very good.

The word of the Lord.

DISCUSSION QUESTIONS

What are your thoughts and feelings as you hear that you are made in the likeness of God and are very good?

How do you, as individuals, reflect God's presence in the world?

How do you image God to each other?

How does your behavior as a couple present a fuller image of God to others?

NOTES

Old Testament Reading Number 102
(Genesis 2:18-24)

A reading from the book of Genesis

The LORD God said: "It is not good for the man to be alone. I will make a suitable partner for him." So the LORD God formed out of the ground various wild animals and various birds of the air, and he brought them to the man to see what he would call them; whatever the man called each of them would be its name. The man gave names to all the cattle, all the birds of the air, and all the wild animals; but none proved to be the suitable partner for the man.

So the LORD God cast a deep sleep on the man, and while he was asleep, he took out one of his ribs and closed up its place with flesh. The LORD God then built up into a woman the rib that he had taken from the man. When he brought her to the man, the man said:

"This one, at last, is bone of my bones
    and flesh of my flesh;
This one shall be called 'woman,'
    for out of 'her man' this one has been taken."

That is why a man leaves his father and mother and clings to his wife, and the two of them become one body.

The word of the Lord.

DISCUSSION QUESTIONS

We have a basic need to belong to other people. How do you seek to fulfill the need to belong with your family, friends, coworkers, community, church, and organizations?

List the joys you have shared during your courtship. How have these joys and their memories contributed to your happiness and decision to marry in the Church?

NOTES

Old Testament Reading Number 103
(Genesis 24:48-51, 58-67)

A reading from the book of Genesis

The servant of Abraham said to Laban: "I bowed down in worship to the LORD, blessing the LORD, the God of my master Abraham, who had led me on the right road to obtain the daughter of my master's kinsman for his son. If, therefore, you have in mind to show true loyalty to my master, let me know; but if not, let me know that, too. I can then proceed accordingly."

Laban and his household said in reply: "This thing comes from the LORD; we can say nothing to you either for or against it. Here is Rebekah, ready for you; take her with you, that she may become the wife of your master's son, as the LORD has said."

So they called Rebekah and asked her, "Do you wish to go with this man?" She answered, "I do." At this they allowed their sister Rebekah and her nurse to take leave, along with Abraham's servant and his men. Invoking a blessing on Rebekah, they said:

"Sister, may you grow
　　into thousands of myriads;
And may your descendants gain possession
　　of the gates of their enemies!"

Then Rebekah and her maids started out; they mounted their camels and followed the man. So the servant took Rebekah and went on his way.

Meanwhile Isaac had gone from Beer-lahai-roi and was living in the region of the Negeb. One day toward evening he went out...in the field, and as he looked around, he noticed that camels were approaching. Rebekah, too, was looking about, and when she saw him, she alighted from her camel and asked the servant, "Who is the man out there, walking through the fields toward us?" "That is my master," replied the servant. Then she covered herself with her veil.

The servant recounted to Isaac all the things he had done. Then Isaac took Rebekah into his tent; he married her, and thus she became his wife. In his love for her Isaac found solace after the death of his mother Sarah.

The word of the Lord.

THE TWO SHALL BE ONE

DISCUSSION QUESTIONS

What first attracted you to each other?

What made you fall more deeply in love with each other?

What role does God have in your life-lived shared love?

NOTES

Old Testament Reading Number 104
(Tobit 7:9-10, 11-15)

A reading from the book of Tobit

Tobiah said to Raphael, "Brother Azariah, ask Raguel to let me marry my kinswoman Sarah." Raguel overheard the words; so he said to the boy: "Eat and drink and be merry tonight, for no man is more entitled to marry my daughter Sarah than you, brother. Besides, not even I have the right to give her to anyone but you, because you are my closest relative. But I will explain the situation to you very frankly....She is yours according to the decree of the Book of Moses. Your marriage to her has been decided in heaven! Take your kinswoman from now on you are her love, and she is your beloved. She is yours today and ever after. And tonight, son, may the Lord of heaven prosper you both. May he grant you mercy and peace." Then Raguel called his daughter Sarah, and she came to him. He took her by the hand and gave her to Tobiah with the words: "Take her according to the law. According to the decree written in the Book of Moses she is your wife. Take her and bring her back safely to your father. And may the God of heaven grant both of you peace and prosperity." He then called her mother and told her to bring a scroll, so that he might draw up a marriage contract stating that he gave Sarah to Tobiah as his wife according to the decree of the Mosaic law. Her mother brought the scroll, and he drew up the contract, to which they affixed their seals.

Afterward they began to eat and drink.

The word of the Lord.

DISCUSSION QUESTIONS

How do your families show support for you?

How might your respective families eventually interfere in your living out the sacrament of matrimony?

How can you share your mutual love for your families?

NOTES

Old Testament Reading Number 105
(Tobit 8:5-7)

A reading from the book of Tobit

On the wedding night Sarah got up, and she and Tobiah started to pray and beg that deliverance might be theirs. He began with these words:

"Blessed are you, O God of our fathers;
   praised be your name forever and ever.
Let the heavens and all your creation
   praise you forever.
You made Adam and you gave him his wife Eve
   to be his help and support;
   and from these two the human race descended.
You said, 'It is not good for the man to be alone;
   let us make him a partner like himself.'
Now, Lord, you know that I take this wife of mine
   not because of lust,
   but for a noble purpose.
Call down your mercy on me and on her,
   and allow us to live together to a happy old age."

The word of the Lord.

DISCUSSION QUESTIONS

How would you describe to each other your personal relationship with God?

How can you enhance your relationship with God and each other through couple prayer?

NOTES

Old Testament Reading Number 106
(Song of Songs 2:8-10, 14, 16; 8:6-7)

A reading from the Song of Songs

Hark! my lover—here he comes
     springing across the mountains,
     leaping across the hills.
My lover is like a gazelle
     or a young stag.
Here he stands behind our wall,
     gazing through the windows,
     peering through the lattices.
My lover speaks; he says to me,
     "Arise, my beloved, my beautiful one,
     and come!
"O my dove in the clefts of the rock,
     in the secret recesses of the cliff,
Let me see you,
     let me hear your voice,
For your voice is sweet,
     and you are lovely."
My lover belongs to me and I to him.
     [He said to me:]
Set me as a seal on your heart,
     as a seal on your arm;
For stern as death is love,
     relentless as the nether world is devotion;
     its flames are a blazing fire.
Deep waters cannot quench love,
     nor floods sweep it away.

The word of the Lord.

DISCUSSION QUESTIONS

*What endearment terms do you have in your love relationship
with God?*

*Do you have a special love poem or song? What about the
poem/song do the two of you like?*

NOTES

Old Testament Reading Number 107
(Sirach 26:1-4, 13-16)

A reading from the book of Sirach

Happy the husband of a good wife,
    twice-lengthened are his days;
A worthy wife brings joy to her husband,
    peaceful and full is his life.
A good wife is a generous gift
    bestowed upon him who fears the LORD;
Be he rich or poor, his heart is content,
    and a smile is ever on his face.
A gracious wife delights her husband,
    her thoughtfulness puts flesh on his bones;
A gift from the LORD is her governed speech,
    and her firm virtue is of surpassing worth.
Choicest of blessings is a modest wife,
    priceless her chaste person.
Like the sun rising in the LORD's heavens,
    the beauty of a virtuous wife is the radiance of her home.

The word of the Lord.

DISCUSSION QUESTIONS

What special qualities do you like about each other?

How will your matrimonial relationship enhance your relationships with friends, coworkers, and your parishioners?

NOTES

Old Testament Reading Number 108
(Jeremiah 31:31-32, 33-34)

A reading from the book of the prophet Jeremiah

The days are coming, says the LORD, when I will make a new covenant with the house of Israel and the house of Judah. It will not be like the covenant I made with their fathers the day I took them by the hand to lead them forth from the land of Egypt....But this is the covenant which I will make with the house of Israel after those days, says the LORD. I will place my law within them, and write it upon their hearts; I will be their God, and they shall be my people. No longer will they have need to teach their friends and kinsmen how to know the Lord. All, from least to greatest, shall know me, says the LORD.

The word of the Lord.

DISCUSSION QUESTIONS

In living the sacrament of matrimony, couples mirror to each other, to the Church, and to the world God's unconditional love for all humankind. Is there anything about each other that you find difficult to accept?

Have each of you addressed this difficulty? How? If not, how do you plan to either address and overcome it or become accepting of it?

When will it be difficult to love each other unconditionally?

NOTES

New Testament Readings

New Testament Reading Number 151
(Romans 8:31-35, 37-39)

A reading from the letter of Paul to the Romans

If God is for us, who can be against us? Is it possible that he who did not spare his own Son but handed him over for the sake of us all will not grant us all things besides? Who shall bring a charge against God's chosen ones? God, who justifies? Who shall condemn them? Christ Jesus, who died or rather was raised up, who is at the right hand of God and intercedes for us?

Who will separate us from the love of Christ? Trial, or distress, or persecution, or hunger, or nakedness, or danger, or the sword? Yet in all this we are more than conquerors because of him who has loved us. For I am certain that neither death nor life, neither angels nor principalities, neither the present nor the future, nor powers, neither height nor depth nor any other creature, will be able to separate us from the love of God that comes to us in Christ Jesus, our Lord.

The word of the Lord.

DISCUSSION QUESTIONS

What might separate you from spending time and sharing life with each other?

What can you do to reassure each other daily that you value the life you share?

How would you define the word "commitment" as it applies to the sacrament of matrimony?

NOTES

New Testament Reading Number 152
(Romans 12:1-2, 9-18 or 12:1-2,9-13)

A reading from the letter of Paul to the Romans

(Long Form)

Brothers, I beg you through the mercy of God to offer your bodies as a living sacrifice holy and acceptable to God, your spiritual worship. Do not conform yourselves to this age but be transformed by the renewal of your mind, so that you may judge what is God's will, what is good, pleasing and perfect.

Your love must be sincere. Detest what is evil, cling to what is good. Love one another with the affection of brothers. Anticipate each other in showing respect. Do not grow slack but be fervent in spirit; he whom you serve is the Lord. Rejoice in hope, be patient under trial, persevere in prayer. Look on the needs of the saints as your own; be generous in offering hospitality. Bless your persecutors; bless and do not curse them. Rejoice with those who rejoice, weep with those who weep. Have the same attitude toward all. Put away ambitious thoughts and associate with those who are lowly. Do not be wise in your own estimation. Never repay injury with injury. See that your conduct is honorable in the eyes of all. If possible, live peaceably with everyone.

The word of the Lord.

(Short Form)

Brothers, I beg you through the mercy of God to offer your bodies as a living sacrifice holy and acceptable to God, your spiritual worship. Do not conform yourselves to this age but be transformed by the renewal of your mind, so that you may judge what is God's will, what is good, pleasing and perfect.

Your love must be sincere. Detest what is evil, cling to what is good. Love one another with the affection of brothers. Anticipate each other in showing respect. Do not grow slack but be fervent in spirit; he whom you serve is the Lord. Rejoice in hope, be patient under trial, persevere in prayer. Look on the needs of the saints as your own; be generous in offering hospitality.

The word of the Lord.

DISCUSSION QUESTIONS

The love you share affects those around you. What positive effects does your shared love bring to others?

As a sacramental couple, how can you share your Christlike love with family, friends, coworkers, and your parish family?

What possible hardships may lie in your future? Are such hardships caused by God? If they actually do occur, do these hardships reflect a lack of God's love for you?

NOTES

New Testament Reading Number 153
(1 Corinthians 6:13-15, 17-20)

A reading from the first letter of Paul to the Corinthians

The body is not for immorality; it is for the Lord, and the Lord is for the body. God, who raised up the Lord, will raise us also by his power.

Do you not see that your bodies are members of Christ? But whoever is joined to the Lord becomes one spirit with him. Shun lewd conduct. Every other sin a man commits is outside his body, but the fornicator sins against his own body. You must know that your body is a temple of the Holy Spirit, who is within—the Spirit you have received from God. You are not your own. You have been purchased, and at what a price. So glorify God in your body.

The word of the Lord.

DISCUSSION QUESTIONS

Your body is a temple of the Holy Spirit. God lives in you and you live in God. In what ways do you show respect for your bodies as temples of the Holy Spirit?

Do you show respect for each other's body and person?

NOTES

New Testament Reading Number 154
(1 Corinthians 12:31–13:8)

 A reading from the first letter of Paul to the Corinthians

Set your hearts on greater gifts. Now I will show you the way which surpasses all the others. If I speak with human tongues and angelic as well, but do not have love, I am a noisy gong, a clanging cymbal. If I have the gift of prophecy and, with full knowledge, comprehend all mysteries, if I have faith great enough to move mountains, but have not love, I am nothing. If I give everything I have to feed the poor and hand over my body to be burned, but have not love, I gain nothing.

Love is patient; love is kind. Love is not jealous, it does not put on airs, it is not snobbish. Love is never rude, it is not self-seeking, it is not prone to anger; neither does it brood over injuries. Love does not rejoice in what is wrong but rejoices with the truth. There is no limit to love's forbearance, to its trust, its hope, its power to endure.

Love never fails.

The word of the Lord.

DISCUSSION QUESTIONS

As hard as we may try, we can never love perfectly, as God loves. What behaviors and words of yours have been unChristlike in your relationship

Are you able to admit your failings? How have you reconciled with each other for grievances you've experienced in your relationship?

How do your past reconciliations mirror the celebration of the sacrament of reconciliation?

NOTES

A reading from the letter of Paul to the Ephesians

(Long Form)

Follow the way of love, even as Christ loved you. He gave himself for us.

Defer to one another out of reverence for Christ.

Wives should be submissive to their husbands as if to the Lord because the husband is head of his wife just as Christ is head of his body the church, as well as its savior. As the church submits to Christ, so wives should submit to their husbands in everything.

Husbands, love your wives, as Christ loved the church. He gave himself up for her to make her holy, purifying her in the bath of water by the power of the word, to present to himself a glorious church, holy and immaculate, without stain or wrinkle or anything of that sort. Husbands should love their wives as they do their own bodies. He who loves his wife loves himself. Observe that no one ever hates his own flesh; no, he nourishes it and takes care of it as Christ cares for the church—for we are members of his body.

> "For this reason a man shall leave his father and mother,
>   and cling to his wife,
>   and the two shall be made into one."

This is a great foreshadowing; I mean that it refers to Christ and the Church. In any case, each one should love his wife as he loves himself, the wife for her part showing respect for her husband.

The word of the Lord.

(Short Form)

Follow the way of love, even as Christ loved you. He gave himself for us.

Husbands, love your wives, as Christ loved the church. He gave himself up for her to make her holy, purifying her in the bath of water by the power of the word, to present to himself a glorious church, holy and immaculate, without stain or wrinkle or anything of that sort. Husbands should love their wives as they do their own bodies. He who loves his wife loves himself. Observe that no one ever hates his own flesh; no, he nourishes it and takes care of it as Christ cares for the church—for we are members of his body.

"For this reason a man shall leave his father and mother,
and cling to his wife,
and the two shall be made into one."

This is a great foreshadowing; I mean that it refers to Christ and the Church.

The word of the Lord.

DISCUSSION QUESTIONS

In what ways do you speak your oneness?

How does your oneness reflect the oneness God wants to have with us?

As a matrimonial couple, in what additional ways will you speak of the oneness and unity you will share?

NOTES

New Testament Reading Number 156
(Colossians 3:12-17)

A reading from the letter of Paul to the Colossians

Because you are God's chosen ones, holy and beloved, clothe yourselves with heartfelt mercy, with kindness, humility, meekness, and patience. Bear with one another; forgive whatever grievances you have against one another. Forgive as the Lord has forgiven you. Over all these virtues put on love, which binds the rest together and makes them perfect. Christ's peace must reign in your hearts, since as members of the one body you have been called to that peace. Dedicate yourselves to thankfulness. Let the word of Christ, rich as it is, dwell in you. In wisdom made perfect, instruct and admonish one another. Sing gratefully to God from your hearts in psalms, hymns, and inspired songs. Whatever you do, whether in speech or in action, do it in the name of the Lord Jesus. Give thanks to God the Father through him.

The word of the Lord.

DISCUSSION QUESTIONS

What are your individual goals through matrimony?

What are your ultimate goals as a matrimonial couple?

What place does God have in your ultimate goals?

NOTES

New Testament Reading Number 157
(1 Peter 3:1-9)

A reading from the first letter of Peter

You married women must obey your husbands, so that any of
them who do not believe in the word of the gospel may be won
over apart from preaching, through their wives' conduct. They
have only to observe the reverent purity of your way of life. The
affectation of an elaborate hairdress, the wearing of golden jewelry,
or the donning of rich robes is not for you. Your adornment is
rather the hidden character of the heart, expressed in the unfading
beauty of a calm and gentle disposition. This is precious in God's
eyes. The holy women of past ages used to adorn themselves in
this way, reliant on God and obedient to their husbands—for
example, Sarah, who was subject to Abraham and called him her
master. You are her children when you do what is right and let no
fears alarm you.

You husbands, too, must show consideration for those who
share your lives. Treat women with respect as the weaker sex,
heirs just as much as you to the gracious gift of life. If you do so,
nothing will keep your prayers from being answered.

In summary, then, all of you should be like-minded, sympa-
thetic, loving toward one another, kindly disposed, and humble.
Do not return evil for evil or insult for insult. Return a blessing
instead. This you have been called to do, that you may receive a
blessing as your inheritance.

The word of the Lord.

DISCUSSION QUESTIONS

*As a woman/man, what unique attributes do you bring to your
relationship?*

*How does your respective maleness/femaleness enhance your
life and relationship?*

NOTES

New Testament Reading Number 158
(1 John 3:18-24)

A reading from the first letter of John

Little children,
let us love in deed and in truth
and not merely talk about it.
This is our way of knowing we are committed to the truth
and are at peace before him
no matter what our consciences may charge us with;
for God is greater than our hearts
and all is known to him.
Beloved,
if our consciences have nothing to charge us with,
we can be sure that God is with us
and that we will receive at his hands
whatever we ask.
Why? Because we are keeping his commandments
and doing what is pleasing in his sight.
His commandment is this:
we are to believe in the name of his Son, Jesus Christ,
and are to love one another as he commanded us.
Those who keep his commandments remain in him
and he in them.
And this is how we know that he remains in us:
from the Spirit that he gave us.

The word of the Lord.

DISCUSSION QUESTIONS

One of the greatest means of experiencing love for each other and God's love for you is through your regular communication about your life? How often do you share your thoughts and feelings about people and events in your life?

How often do you talk about your thoughts and feelings for each other?

What elements of your conversations, such as honesty, openness, ability to listen, and sincerity, contribute to successful communication between you?

Which of the above elements are strong characteristics of your individual communication styles? Which elements do you each need to work on?

NOTES

New Testament Reading Number 159
(1 John 4:7-12)

A reading from the first letter of John

Beloved,
let us love one another,
because love is of God;
everyone who loves is begotten of God
and has knowledge of God.
The man without love has known nothing of God,
for God is love.
God's love was revealed in our midst in this way:
he sent his only Son to the world
that we might have life through him.
Love, then, consists in this:
not that we have loved God
but that he has loved us
and has sent his Son as an offering for our sins.
Beloved,
if God has loved us so,
we must have the same love for one another.
No one has ever seen God.
Yet if we love one another
God dwells in us,
and his love is brought to perfection in us.

The word of the Lord.

DISCUSSION QUESTIONS

How have you made God as love present to each other?

When we love, we make Christ's love visible in the world. What thoughts and feelings does that statement evoke in each of you?

NOTES

New Testament Reading Number 160
(Revelation 19:1, 5-9)

A reading from the book of Revelation

After this I [John] heard what sounded like the loud song of a great assembly in heaven. They were singing:

"Alleluia!
Salvation, glory, and might belong to our God."

A voice coming from the throne cried out:

"Praise our God, all you his servants,
the small and the great, who revere him!"

Then I heard what sounded like the shouts of a great crowd, or the roaring of the deep, or mighty peals of thunder, as they cried:

"Alleluia!
The Lord is king,
our God, the Almighty!
Let us rejoice and be glad,
and gave him glory!
For this is the wedding day of the Lamb,
his bride has prepared herself for the wedding.
She has been given a dress to wear
made of finest linen, brilliant white."

(The linen dress is the virtuous deeds of God's saints.)

The angel then said to me: "Write this down: Happy are they who have been invited to the wedding feast of the Lamb."

The word of the Lord.

DISCUSSION QUESTIONS

How will your wedding reception speak of your love for God and each other and your shared Christian values?

Reflecting on your own dreams for your wedding celebration, what insights do you have regarding the heavenly wedding feast God has in store for all faithful servants?

NOTES

Responsorial Psalms

Responsorial Psalm Number 201
(Psalm 33:12, 18, 20-21, 22)
R. The earth is full of the goodness of the Lord.

Happy the nation whose God is the Lord,
    the people he has chosen for his own inheritance.
But see, eyes of the Lord are upon those who fear him,
    upon those who hope for his kindness.

R. The earth is full of the goodness of the Lord.

Our soul waits for the Lord,
    who is our help and our shield,
For in him our hearts rejoice;
    in his holy name we trust.

R. The earth is full of the goodness of the Lord.

May your kindness, O Lord, be upon us
    who have put our hope in you.

R. The earth is full of the goodness of the Lord.

Responsorial Psalm Number 202
(Psalm 34:2-3, 4-5, 6-7, 8-9)
R. I will bless the Lord at all times.
(Or: Taste and see the goodness of the Lord.)

I will bless the Lord at all times;
    his praise shall be ever in my mouth.
Let my soul glory in the Lord;
    the lowly will hear me and be glad.

R. I will bless the Lord at all times.
(Or: Taste and see the goodness of the Lord.)

Glorify the Lord with me,
    let us together extol his name.

I sought the Lord, and he answered me
and delivered me from all my fears.

R. **I will bless the Lord at all times.**
(Or: Taste and see the goodness of the Lord.)

Look to him that you may be radiant with joy,
and your faces may not blush with shame.
When the afflicted man called out, the Lord heard,
and from all his distress he saved him.

R. **I will bless the Lord at all times.**
(Or: Taste and see the goodness of the Lord.)

The angel of the Lord encamps
around those who fear him, and delivers them.
Taste and see how good the Lord is;
happy the man who takes refuge in him.

R. **I will bless the Lord at all times.**
(Or: Taste and see the goodness of the Lord.)

**Responsorial Psalm Number 203
(Psalm 103:1-2, 8, 13, 17-18)**
R. **The Lord is kind and merciful.**
(Or: The Lord's kindness is everlasting to those who fear him.)

Bless the Lord, O my soul;
and all my being, bless his holy name.
Bless the Lord, O my soul,
and forget not all his benefits.

R. **The Lord is kind and merciful.**
(Or: The Lord's kindness is everlasting to those who fear him.)

Merciful and gracious is the Lord,
slow to anger and abounding in kindness.
As a father has compassion on his children,
so the Lord has compassion on those who fear him.

R. **The Lord is kind and merciful.**
(Or: The Lord's kindness is everlasting to those who fear him.)

But the kindness of the Lord is from eternity
    to eternity toward those who fear him,
And his justice toward children's children
    among those who keep his covenant.

R. **The Lord is kind and merciful.**
(Or: The Lord's kindness is everlasting to those who fear him.)

Responsorial Psalm Number 204
(Psalm 112:1-2, 3-4, 5-7, 7-8, 9)
R. **Happy are those who do what the Lord commands.**
(Or: Alleluia.)

Happy the man who fears the Lord,
    who greatly delights in his commands.
His posterity shall be mighty upon the earth;
    the upright generation shall be blessed.

R. **Happy are those who do what the Lord commands.**
(Or: Alleluia.)

Wealth and riches shall be in his house;
    his generosity shall endure forever.
He dawns through the darkness, a light for the upright;
    he is gracious and merciful and just.

R. **Happy are those who do what the Lord commands.**
(Or: Alleluia.)

Well for the man who is gracious and lends,
    who conducts his affairs with justice;
He shall never be moved;
    the just man shall be in everlasting remembrance.

R. **Happy are those who do what the Lord commands.**
(Or: Alleluia.)

An evil report he shall not fear.
His heart is firm, trusting in the Lord.
His heart is steadfast; he shall not fear
till he looks down upon his foes.

R. **Happy are those who do what the Lord commands.**
(Or: Alleluia.)

Lavishly he gives to the poor;
his generosity shall endure forever;
his horn shall be exalted in glory.

R. **Happy are those who do what the Lord commands.**
(Or: Alleluia.)

Responsorial Psalm Number 205
(Psalm 128:1-2, 3, 4-5)

R. **Happy are those who fear the Lord.**
(Or: See how the Lord blesses those who fear him.)

Happy are you who fear the Lord,
who walk in his ways!
For you shall eat the fruit of your handiwork;
happy shall you be, and favored.

R. **Happy are those who fear the Lord.**
(Or: See how the Lord blesses those who fear him.)

Your wife shall be like a fruitful vine
in the recesses of your home;
Your children like olive plants
around your table.

R. **Happy are those who fear the Lord.**
(Or: See how the Lord blesses those who fear him.)

Behold, thus is the man blessed
who fears the Lord.
The Lord bless you from Sion:
may you see the prosperity of Jerusalem
all the days of your life.

R. Happy are those who fear the Lord.
(Or: See how the Lord blesses those who fear him.)

Responsorial Psalm Number 206
(Psalm 145:8-9, 10, 15, 17-18)
R. The Lord is compassionate to all his creatures.

The Lord is gracious and merciful,
    slow to anger and of great kindness.
The Lord is good to all
    and compassionate toward all his works.

R. The Lord is compassionate to all his creatures.

Let all your works give you thanks, O Lord,
    and let your faithful ones bless you.
The eyes of all look hopefully to you,
    and you give them their food in due season.

R. The Lord is compassionate to all his creatures.

The Lord is just in all his ways
    and holy in all his works.
The Lord is near to all who call upon him,
    to all who call upon him in truth.

R. The Lord is compassionate to all his creatures.

Responsorial Psalm Number 207
(Psalm 148:1-2, 3-4, 9-10, 11-12, 12-14)
R. Let all praise the name of the Lord.

Praise the Lord from the heavens,
    praise him in the heights;
Praise him, all you his angels,
    praise him, all you his hosts.

R. Let all praise the name of the Lord.

Praise him, sun and moon;
    praise him, all you shining stars.
Praise him, you highest heavens,
    and you waters above the heavens.

R. Let all praise the name of the Lord.

You mountains and all you hills,
    you fruit trees and all you cedars;
You wild beasts and all tame animals,
    you creeping things and you winged fowl.

R. Let all praise the name of the Lord.

Let the kings of the earth and all peoples,
    the princes and all the judges of the earth,
Young men too, and maidens,
    old men and boys.

R. Let all praise the name of the Lord.

Praise the name of the Lord,
    for his name alone is exalted;
His majesty is above earth and heaven,
    and he has lifted up the horn of his people.

R. Let all praise the name of the Lord.

Gospel Readings

Gospel Reading Number 251
(Matthew 5:1-12)

A reading from the holy gospel according to Matthew

When Jesus saw the crowds he went up on the mountainside.
After he had sat down his disciples gathered around him, and he
began to teach them:

"How blest are the poor in spirit:
  the reign of God is theirs.
Blest too are the sorrowing;
  they shall be consoled.
[Blest are the lowly;
  they shall inherit the land.]
Blest are they who hunger and thirst for holiness;
  they shall have their fill.
Blest are they who show mercy;
  mercy shall be theirs.
Blest are the single-hearted
  for they shall see God.
Blest too the peacemakers;
  they shall be called sons of God.
Blest are those persecuted for holiness' sake;
  the reign of God is theirs.
Blest are you when they insult you and
  persecute you and utter every kind of
  slander against you because of me.
Be glad and rejoice, for your reward
  is heaven in great."

The gospel of the Lord.

DISCUSSION QUESTION

What are Christlike attitudes of an engaged couple?

NOTES

Gospel Reading Number 252
(Matthew 5:13-16)

A reading from the holy gospel according to Matthew

Jesus said to his disciples: "You are the salt of the earth. But what if salt goes flat? How can you restore its flavor? Then it is good for nothing but to be thrown out and trampled underfoot.

"You are the light of the world. A city set on a hill cannot be hidden. Men do not light a lamp and then put it under a bushel basket. They set it on a stand where it gives light to all in the house. In the same way, your light must shine before men so that they may see goodness in your acts and give praise to your heavenly Father."

The gospel of the Lord.

DISCUSSION QUESTIONS

How do your intentions to enter the sacrament of matrimony speak to your family and friends about your belief in Jesus Christ and your membership in our Catholic Church family?

How can you as a matrimonial couple be salt for the earth and light to the world?

NOTES

Gospel Reading Number 253
(Matthew 7:21,24-29 or 7:21, 24-25)

A reading from the holy gospel according to Matthew

(Long Form)

Jesus said to his disciples: "None of those who cry out, 'Lord, Lord,' will enter the kingdom of God but only the one who does the will of my Father in heaven.

"Anyone who hears my words and puts them into practice is like a wise man who built his house on rock. When the rainy season set in, the torrents came and the winds blew and buffeted his house. It did not collapse; it had been solidly set on rock. Anyone who hears my words but does not put them into practice is like the foolish man who built his house on sandy ground. The rains fell, the torrents came, the winds blew and lashed against his house. It collapsed under all this and was completely ruined."

Jesus finished this discourse and left the crowds spellbound at his teaching. The reason was that he taught with authority and not like the scribes.

The gospel of the Lord.

(Short Form)

Jesus said to his disciples: "None of those who cry out, 'Lord, Lord,' will enter the kingdom of God but only the one who does the will of my Father in heaven.

"Anyone who hears my words and puts them into practice is like a wise man who built his house on rock. When the rainy season set in, the torrents came and the winds blew and buffeted his house. It did not collapse; it had been solidly set on rock."

The gospel of the Lord.

DISCUSSION QUESTIONS

What strengths from your relationship with God can you rely upon as a married couple?

What strengths in your Catholic community may you call upon during difficult times?

How can you, as a matrimonial couple, be a source of strength

Final Liturgy Sheet

Wedding Ceremony Without a Mass

(Trnasfer the information on your work sheet to this sheet and give this completed form to the presiding minister.)

Groom's Full Name: _____

Work number: _____ Home number: _____
Groom's mother's first and last name:

_____

Groom's father's first and last name:

_____

Bride's Full Name: _____

Work number: _____ Home number: _____
Bride's mother's first and last name:

_____

Bride's father's first and last name:

_____

Wedding Date: ____/____/_____ Time: _____
Rehearsal Date: ____/____/____ Time: _____

Best Man's full name: _____

Maid or matron of honor's full name: _____
Names of the wedding party:

    Groomsmen   Bridesmaids

Names of ushers besides the groomsmen listed above:

_____

Ring bearer: _____

Flower girl(s): _____

Altar server(s): _____

Name of musician(s): _____

_____

Refer to your "Work Sheet" and record the appropriate selections for each of the following areas:

Summarize all you hear God saying in the readings.

ENTRANCE PROCESSION

List the names of grandparents and who will escort them in. What music will accompany them?

Describe the processional order (review options on pages 68-69) of the liturgical ministers, wedding party, and bride and groom. What music will accompany them?

(To the presiding minister: The last digit of each selected prayer, blessing, readings, and vows corresponds to the numbering system in the Sacramentary and Lectionary.)

Opening prayer Number (circle one): 301   302   303   304

READINGS

First reading:

 Old Testament Number: _____

 New Testament Number: _____

 (Where applicable) _____ Long form _____ Short form

Reading to be proclaimed by: _____

Responsorial psalm:

 Sung Responsorial:

 If not sung, we want number: _____

Responsorial psalm to be proclaimed by: _____

Second Reading:

 New Testament Number: _____

 (Where applicable) _____ Long form _____ Short form

Reading to be proclaimed by: _____

Final Liturgy Sheet

Wedding Ceremony With a Mass

(Transfer the information on your work sheet to this sheet and give this completed form to the presiding minister.)

Groom's Full Name: _____

Work number: _____ Home number: _____

Groom's mother's first and last name:

_____

Groom's father's first and last name:

_____

Bride's Full Name: _____

Work number: _____ Home number: _____

Bride's mother's first and last name:

_____

Bride's father's first and last name:

_____

Wedding Date: ____/____/____ Time: _____
Rehearsal Date: ____/____/____ Time: _____

Best Man's full name: _____

Maid or matron of honor's full name: _____

Names of the wedding party:

    Groomsmen   Bridesmaids

Names of ushers besides the groomsmen listed above:

_____

Ring bearer: _____

Flower girl(s): _____

Altar server(s): _____

Name of musician(s): _____

_____

Refer to your "Work Sheet" and record the appropriate selections for each of the following areas:

Summarize all you hear God saying in the readings.

ENTRANCE PROCESSION

List the names of grandparents and who will escort them in. What music will accompany them?

Describe the processional order (review options on pages 68-69) of the liturgical ministers, the wedding party, and the bride and groom. What music will accompany them?

(To the presiding minister: The last digit of each selected prayer, blessing, readings, and vows corresponds to the numbering system in the Sacramentary and Lectionary.)

Opening prayer Number (circle one): 301   302   303   304

READINGS

First reading:

Old Testament Number: _____

New Testament Number: _____

(Where applicable) _____ Long form _____ Short form

Reading to be proclaimed by: _____

Responsorial psalm:

Sung Responsorial:

If not sung, we want number: _____

Responsorial psalm to be proclaimed by: _____

Second Reading:

New Testament Number: _____

(Where applicable) _____ Long form _____ Short form

Reading to be proclaimed by: _____

Work Sheet

Wedding Ceremony Without a Mass
(Detach and use to record your choices.)

READINGS

We want: _____ 2 readings _____ 3 readings

First reading (pages 9-18 and 19-31):

    Old Testament Number: _____

    New Testament Number: _____

    (Where applicable) _____ Long form _____ Short form

Responsorial psalm (pages 32-37):
    If not sung, we want number: _____

Second reading (pages 19-31):

    New Testament Number: _____

    (Where applicable) _____ Long form _____ Short form

Gospel reading (pages 38-49) Number: _____

    (Where applicable) _____ Long form _____ Short form

Focusing on Your Choices (page 50):

How would you summarize all you hear God saying in the readings?

ADDITIONAL SELECTIONS

Opening prayer (pages 52-53) Number (circle one):

      301   302   303   304

Nuptial blessing (pages 56-59) Number (circle one):

      601   602   603

Final blessing (pages 60-63) Number (circle one):

      801   802   803   804

GENERAL INTERCESSIONS
(PAGES 63-64)

There should be four to six general intercessions, presented as requests for things you and your faith community desire from God. General intercessions are NOT prayers of thanksgiving. One general intercession must be for the general Church.

The general intercessions will be:

1)

2)

3)

4)

5)

MARRIAGE VOWS

Vow Option (pages 65-66) Number (circle one): 901   902

Exchange of vows (check one):

   _____ We will memorize our vows.

   _____ We will repeat our vows after the minister.

   _____ We will have the minister present the vows to us, to which we'll respond "I do."

BLESSING OF RINGS

Ring blessing (pages 66-67) Number (circle one):

      1001   1002   1003

One _____ Two _____ ring(s) will be exchanged.

Exchange of rings (check one):

   _____ We will memorize the prayer.

   _____ We will repeat the prayer after the minister.

Work Sheet

Wedding Ceremony With a Mass

(Detach and use to record your wedding Mass choices.)

READINGS

We want: _____ 2 readings _____ 3 readings

First reading (pages 9-18 and 19-31):

    Old Testament Number: _____

    New Testament Number: _____

    (Where applicable) _____ Long form _____ Short form

Responsorial psalm (pages 32-37):
    If not sung, we want number: _____

Second reading (pages 19-31):

    New Testament Number: _____

    (Where applicable) _____ Long form _____ Short form

Gospel reading (pages 38-49) Number: _____

    (Where applicable) _____ Long form _____ Short form

Focusing on Your Choices (page 50):

How would you summarize all you hear God saying in the readings?

ADDITIONAL EUCHARISTIC SELECTIONS

Opening prayer (pages 52-53) Number (circle one):

    301   302   303   304

Prayer over the gifts (pages 53-54) Number (circle one):

    401   402   403

Preface (pages 54-55) Number (circle one):

    501   502   503

Nuptial blessing (pages 56-59) Number (circle one):

    601   602   603

Prayer after Communion (pages 59-60) Number (circle one):

    701   702   703

Final blessing (pages 60-63) Number (circle one):

    801   802   803   804

GENERAL INTERCESSIONS
(PAGES 63-64)

There should be four to six general intercessions, presented as requests for things you and your faith community desire from God. General intercessions are NOT prayers of thanksgiving. One general intercession must be for the general Church.

The general intercessions will be:

1)

2)

3)

4)

5)

MARRIAGE VOWS

Vow Option (pages 65-66) Number (circle one): 901   902

Exchange of vows (check one):

_____ We will memorize our vows.

___X___ We will repeat our vows after the minister.

_____ We will have the minister present the vows to us, to which we'll respond "I do."

BLESSING OF RINGS

Ring blessing (pages 66-67) Number (circle one):

          1001   1002   1003

One _____ Two _____ ring(s) will be exchanged.

Exchange of rings (check one):

_____ We will memorize the prayer.

___X___ We will repeat the prayer after the minister.

OTHER CEREMONIAL OPTIONS
(PAGES 68-73)

How and when will we receive our guests?

How do we want to process in?

Who might we ask to proclaim the readings?

A unity candle?

Who will present the gifts of bread and wine?

Who do we know that are eucharistic ministers?

Should we honor Mary and how?

Should we have a receiving line? When and where?

FURTHER CEREMONIAL CONSIDERATIONS
(PAGES 74-76)

What type of pictures do we want taken?

Where and when should pictures be taken?

Do we want to have a wedding booklet?

Who has to be at the rehearsal?

NOTES

OTHER CEREMONIAL OPTIONS
(PAGES 68-73)

How and when will we receive our guests?

How do we want to process in?

Who might we ask to proclaim the readings?

A unity candle?

Should we honor Mary and how?

Should we have a receiving line? When and where?

FURTHER CEREMONIAL CONSIDERATIONS
(PAGES 74-76)

What type of pictures do we want taken?

Where and when should pictures be taken?

Do we want to have a wedding booklet?

Who has to be at the rehearsal?

NOTES

Gospel: Proclaimed by the priest or deacon.

    Sung gospel acclamation:

    Reading Number: _____

    (Where applicable) _____ Long form _____ Short form

MARRIAGE VOWS

Vow option number (circle one): 901   902

Exchange of vows (check one):

    _____ We will memorize our vows.

    _____ We will repeat our vows after the minister.

    _____ We will have the minister present the vows to us,
        to which we'll respond "I do."

BLESSING OF RINGS

Ring blessing Number (circle one): 1001   1002   1003

We will exchange: One ring   Two rings

When exchanging rings (check one):

    _____ We will memorize the prayer.

    _____ We will repeat the prayer after the minister.

GENERAL INTERCESSIONS

The general intercessions will be:

1)

2)

3)

4)

5)

General intercessions will be read by: _____

GIFTS AND GIFT PRESENTERS

Names of gift presenters: _____

_____

Presentation music: _____

Prayer over the gifts Number (circle one):   401   402   403

Preface Number (circle one):   501   502   503

Holy to be sung: _____

Memorial Acclamation to be sung: _____

Amen to be sung: _____

Nuptial blessing Number (circle one):   601   602   603

If sung, Lamb of God: _____

COMMUNION

Communion music: _____

Eucharistic ministers (check one):

_____ Parish should provide.   _____ We will provide.

Eucharistic ministers will be (list names):

_____

Prayer after Communion Number (circle one):   701   702   703

Final blessing Number (circle one): 801   802   803   804

Recessional music: _____

Other comments or special plans for the ceremony (plans to greet guests as they arrive or a reception line, unity candle, Marian devotion, additional music):

Gospel: Proclaimed by the priest or deacon.

Sung gospel acclamation: _____

    Reading Number: _____

    (Where applicable) _____ Long form   _____ Short form

MARRIAGE VOWS

Vow option number (circle one): 901   902

Exchange of vows (check one):

    _____ We will memorize our vows.

    _____ We will repeat our vows after the minister.

    _____ We will have the minister present the vows to us,
        to which we'll respond "I do."

BLESSING OF RINGS

Ring blessing number (circle one): 1001   1002   1003

We will exchange: One ring   Two rings

When exchanging rings (check one):

    _____ We will memorize the prayer.

    _____ We will repeat the prayer after the minister.

GENERAL INTERCESSIONS

The general intercessions will be:

1)

2)

3)

4)

5)

General intercessions will be read by: _____

Nuptial blessing Number (circle one):

601   602   603

Final blessing Number (circle one):

801   802   803   804

Recessional music: _____

Other comments or special plans for the ceremony (plans to greet guests as they arrive or a reception line, unity candle, Marian devotion, additional music):

Music Planning Guide

for Weddings With a Mass

Not all the areas listed below need musical enhancement. This listing should assist you and your musician to discuss and prepare musical choices for your celebration.

PRELUDE

PROCESSIONAL

Music for the procession of grandparents and/or parents, liturgical ministers, the wedding party, and the bride (and groom):

Gathering song: _____

LITURGY OF THE WORD

Responsorial psalm: _____

Gospel acclamation: _____

LITURGY OF THE EUCHARIST

Preparation and presentation of gifts:

_____

Holy, Holy: _____

Memorial Acclamation: _____

Great Amen: _____

Lamb of God: _____

Communion song: _____

Recessional song: _____

ADDITIONAL MUSICAL CONSIDERATIONS

Music Planning Guide

for Weddings Without a Mass

Not all the areas listed below need musical enhancement. This listing should assist you and your musician to discuss and prepare musical choices for your celebration.

PRELUDE

PROCESSIONAL

Music for the procession of grandparents and/or parents, liturgical ministers, the wedding party, and the bride (and groom):

Gathering song: _____

LITURGY OF THE WORD

Responsorial psalm: _____

Gospel acclamation: _____

Recessional song: _____

ADDITIONAL MUSICAL CONSIDERATIONS

to members of your Catholic community in their moments of need and struggle?

NOTES

Gospel Reading Number 254
(Matthew 19:3-6)

A reading from the holy gospel according to Matthew

Some Pharisees came up to Jesus and said, to test him, "May a man divorce his wife for any reason whatever?" He replied, "Have you not read that at the beginning the Creator made them male and female and declared, 'For this reason a man shall leave his father and mother and cling to his wife, and the two shall become as one'? Thus they are no longer two but one flesh. Therefore, let no man separate what God has joined."

The gospel of the Lord.

DISCUSSION QUESTIONS

Not all Christian churches view married life as a sacrament; they recognize divorce. What measures can the two of you take to safeguard your special sacrament of love?

How can you support and encourage other sacramental couples in your parish and among your friendships to remain faithful to their special calling from God?

NOTES

Gospel Reading Number 255
(Matthew 22:35-40)

A reading from the holy gospel according to Matthew

One of the Pharisees, a lawyer, in an attempt to trip up Jesus, asked him, "Teacher, which commandment of the law is the greatest?" Jesus said to him:

"'You shall love the Lord your God
with your whole heart,
with your whole soul,
and with all your mind.'

This is the greatest and first commandment. The second is like it:
'You shall love your neighbor as yourself.'
On these two commandments the whole law is based, and the prophets as well."

The gospel of the Lord.

DISCUSSION QUESTIONS

What can you do to help each other develop a greater love for God?

What can your parish do for you to strengthen your love for God?

What can you do for your fellow parishioners to strengthen their love for God?

NOTES

Gospel Reading Number 256
(Mark 10:6-9)

A reading from the holy gospel according to Mark

Jesus said: "At the beginning of creation God made them male and female; for this reason a man shall leave his father and mother and the two shall become as one. They are no longer two but one flesh. Therefore let no man separate what God has joined."

The gospel of the Lord.

DISCUSSION QUESTIONS

What specific behaviors display the oneness you intend to share with each other?

How much of a say does God have in your decisions to have children, a visible sign of your oneness?

If you are/were incapable of having children, how would this impact your matrimonial relationship and your relationship with God?

NOTES

Gospel Reading Number 257
(John 2:1-11)

A reading from the holy gospel according to John

There was a wedding at Cana in Galilee, and the mother of Jesus was there. Jesus and his disciples had likewise been invited to the celebration. At a certain point the wine ran out, and Jesus' mother told him, "They have no more wine." Jesus replied, "Woman, how does this concern of yours involve me? My hour has not yet come." His mother instructed those waiting on table, "Do whatever he tells you." As prescribed for Jewish ceremonial washings, there were at hand six stone water jars, each one holding fifteen to twenty-five gallons. "Fill those jars with water," Jesus ordered, at which they filled them to the brim. "Now," he said, "draw some out and take it to the waiter in charge." They did as he instructed them. The waiter in charge tasted the water made wine, without knowing where it had come from; only the waiters knew, since they had drawn the water. Then the waiter in charge called the groom over and remarked to him: "People usually serve the choice wine first; then when the guests have been drinking awhile, a lesser vintage. What you have done is keep the choice wine until now." Jesus performed this first of his signs at Cana in Galilee. Thus did he reveal his glory, and his disciples believed in him.

The gospel of the Lord.

DISCUSSION QUESTIONS

How would you feel if you ran out of beverages at your wedding reception?

How big does a concern have to be for the two of you to turn to God with it?

Have you ever prayed before having a fight?

NOTES

Gospel Reading Number 258
(John 15:9-12)

X A reading from the holy gospel according to John

Jesus said to his disciples:
    "As the Father has loved me,
    so I have loved you.
    Live on in my love.
    You will live in my love
    if you keep my commandments,
    even as I have kept my Father's commandments,
    and live in his love.
    All this I tell you
    that my joy may be yours
    and your joy may be complete.
    This is my commandment:
    love one another
    as I have loved you."

                The gospel of the Lord.

DISCUSSION QUESTIONS

Often times it's the little things spouses do for each other that make their love visible. What little things do you do for each other?

What little things do you plan to do for each other as husband and wife to make your love visible?

In light of Jesus' command to "love one another as I have loved you," how might you make your love for each other more Christlike?

NOTES

Gospel Reading Number 259
(John 15:12-16)

A reading from the holy gospel according to John

Jesus said to his disciples:
"This is my commandment:
love one another
as I have loved you.
There is no greater love than this:
to lay down one's life for one's friends.
You are my friends
if you do what I command you.
I no longer speak of you as slaves,
for a slave does not know what his master is about.
Instead, I call you friends,
since I have made known to you all that I
heard from my Father.
It was not you who chose me,
it was I who chose you
to go forth and bear fruit.
Your fruit must endure,
so that all you ask the Father in my name
he will give you."

The gospel of the Lord.

DISCUSSION QUESTIONS

During your courtship and engagement, when have you placed each other's wants and desires first?

Out of love for us, Jesus laid down his life for his friends, for us. In what ways do you lay down your life for each other?

NOTES

Gospel Reading Number 260
(John 17:20-26 or 17:20-23)

A reading from the holy gospel according to John

(Long Form)
Jesus looked up to heaven and prayed:
    "Holy Father,
    I do not pray for my disciples alone.
    I pray also for those who will believe in me
     through their word,
    that all may be one
    as you, Father, are in me, and I in you;
    I pray that they may be [one] in us,
    that the world may believe that you sent me.
    I have given them the glory you gave me
    that they may be one, as we are one—
    I living in them, you living in me—
    that their unity may be complete.
    So shall the world know that you sent me,
    and that you loved them as you loved me.
    Father,
    all those you gave me
    I would have in my company
    where I am,
    to see this glory of mine
    which is your gift to me,
    because of the love you bore me before the world began.
    Just Father,
    the world has not known you,
    but I have known you;
    and these men have known that you sent me.
    To them I have revealed your name,
    and I will continue to reveal it
    so that your love for me may live in them,
    and I may live in them."

                      The gospel of the Lord.

(Short Form)
Jesus looked up to heaven and prayed:
    "Holy Father,
    I do not pray for my disciples alone.

THE TWO SHALL BE ONE

I pray also for those who will believe in me
 through their word,
that all may be one
as you, Father, are in me, and I in you;
I pray that they may be [one] in us,
that the world may believe that you sent me.
I have given them the glory you gave me
that they may be one, as we are one—
I living in them, you living in me—
that their unity may be complete.
So shall the world know that you sent me,
and that you loved them as you loved me."

The gospel of the Lord.

DISCUSSION QUESTIONS

*How has your experience of being one with each other given
you insight into the oneness God wants to share with you?*

*How has your experience of being one with each other given
you insight into the oneness God wants us to share with one
another as God's people, a parish community?*

NOTES

Focusing on Your Choices

A Single Theme

After chosing your readings, review each one separately. Summarize what you hear God saying to you. Look at each summary, and tie all the readings together into a single theme that reflects what God is speaking to you.

For example, let's assume that you decide to have three readings. The first reading is 101 from Genesis. Your summary might be "We reflect the likeness of God to other people and them to us."

Your second reading might be 155, the Letter to the Ephesians, which could be summarized, "Doing things for other people out of love, we make God's love present and real to them."

The gospel you choose may be 256 from Mark. That reading might be summarized as "God's plan for us as a couple is to be united. God's plan for all people is to be united and to work as a unit in our concern and care for one another."

Tying all three readings together, you might summarize the focus of your readings as "God is love and God made us in God's image and likeness. God wants to be one with us. In the sacrament of matrimony, we are called to mirror God's love and God's desire to be one with us. We need to work at our couple love and our love for God's people so God's love will become visible through us as individuals, as a couple, and as a Church."

The summary and focus of your readings make your other selections easier. Don't take this exercise lightly.

What do you hear God saying in the first reading?

*If you choose to have a second reading, what do you hear
God saying in that reading?*

What do you hear God saying in the gospel reading?

Summarize all you hear God saying through the readings.

*Record your choices and the focus of your readings in the
appropriate place on your work sheet.*

Additional Eucharistic Selections

Opening Prayer

Refer to the focus of your readings, which you noted on the appropriate work sheet. Choose an opening prayer that best reflects that summary. If more than one prayer fits, choose the one you like best. Record your decision on the work sheet.

301
Father,
you have made the bond of marriage
a holy mystery,
a symbol of Christ's love for his Church.
Hear our prayers for N. and N.
With faith in you and in each other
they pledge their love today.
May their lives always bear witness
to the reality of that love.

We ask this through our Lord Jesus Christ, your Son,
who lives and reigns with you and the Holy Spirit,
one God, for ever and ever.

302
Father,
hear our prayers for N. and N.,
who today are united in marriage before your altar.
Give them your blessing,
and strengthen their love for each other.

We ask this through our Lord Jesus Christ...

303
Almighty God,
hear our prayers for N. and N.,
who have come here today
to be united in the sacrament of marriage.
Increase their faith in you and in each other,

and through them bless your Church
(with Christian children).

We ask this through our Lord Jesus Christ...

304
Father,
when you created mankind
you willed that man and wife should be one.
Bind N. and N.
in the loving union of marriage;
and make their love fruitful
so that they may be living witnesses
to your divine love in the world.

We ask this through our Lord Jesus Christ...

Prayer Over the Gifts

Refer to the focus of your readings, which you noted on the appropriate work sheet. Choose a prayer over the gifts that best reflects that summary. If more than one prayer fits, choose the one you like best. Record your decision on the work sheet.

401
Lord,
accept our offering
for this newly-married couple, N. and N.
By your love and providence you have brought them together;
now bless them all the days of their married life.

We ask this through Christ our Lord.

402
Lord,
accept the gifts we offer you
on this happy day.
In your fatherly love
watch over and protect N. and N.,
whom you have united in marriage.

We ask this through Christ our Lord.

403

Lord,
hear our prayers
and accept the gifts we offer for N. and N.
Today you have made them one in the sacrament of marriage.
May the mystery of Christ's unselfish love,
which we celebrate in this eucharist,
increase their love for you and for each other.

We ask this through Christ our Lord.

Preface

Refer to the focus of your readings, which you noted on the
appropriate work sheet. Choose a preface for the eucharistic
prayer that best reflects that summary. If more than one preface
fits, choose the one you like best. Record your decision on the
work sheet.

501

Father, all-powerful and ever-living God,
we do well always and everywhere to give you thanks.
By this sacrament your grace unites man and woman
in an unbreakable bond of love and peace.

You have designed the chaste love of husband and wife
for the increase both of the human family
and of your own family born in baptism.
You are the loving Father of the world of nature;
you are the loving Father of the new creation of grace.
In Christian marriage you bring together the two orders of
    creation:
nature's gift of children enriches the world
and your grace enriches also your Church.

Through Christ the choirs of angels
and all the saints
praise and worship your glory.
May our voices blend with theirs
as we join in their unending hymn:

502

Father, all-powerful and ever-living God,
we do well always and everywhere to give you thanks
through Jesus Christ our Lord.

Through him you entered into a new covenant with your people.
You restored man to grace in the saving mystery of redemption.
You gave him a share in the divine life
through his union with Christ.
You made him an heir of Christ's eternal glory.

This outpouring of love in the new covenant of grace
is symbolized in the marriage covenant
that seals the love of husband and wife
and reflects your divine plan of love.

And so, with the angels and all the saints in heaven
we proclaim your glory
and join in their unending hymn of praise:

503

Father, all powerful and ever-living God,
we do well always and everywhere to give you thanks.

You created man in love to share your divine life.
We see his high destiny in the love of husband and wife,
which bears the imprint of your own divine love.

Love is man's origin,
love is his constant calling,
love is his fulfillment in heaven.
The love of man and woman
is made holy in the sacrament of marriage,
and becomes the mirror of your everlasting love.

Through Christ the choirs of angels
and all the saints
praise and worship your glory.
May our voices blend with theirs
as we join in their unending hymn:

Nuptial Blessing

At a wedding with a Mass, the prayer "Deliver us…," which follows the Our Father, is omitted. The minister faces the newly married couple and prays one of the following three blessings.

At a wedding without a Mass, the prayers of the faithful are concluded with the nuptial blessing.

Refer to the focus of your readings, which you noted on the appropriate work sheet. Choose a nuptial blessing that best reflects that summary. If more than one blessing fits, choose the one you like best. Record your decision on the work sheet.

601

My dear friends, let us turn to the Lord and pray
that he will bless with his grace this woman (or N.)
now married in Christ to this man (or N.)
and that
(through the sacrament of the body and blood of Christ,)
he will unite in love the couple he has joined in this holy bond.

All pray silently for a short while. Then the priest extends his hands and continues.

NOTE: if one or both of the parties will not be receiving communion, the words "through the sacrament of the body and blood of Christ" will be omitted.

There are three paragraphs that begin "Father…." The "Father" paragraph that best corresponds with your readings will be used.

In the last paragraph, the words in parentheses should be omitted whenever circumstances suggest, for example, if the couple is beyond childbearing years.

Father, by your power you have made everything out of nothing.
In the beginning you created the universe
and made mankind in your own likeness.
You gave man the constant help of woman
so that man and woman should no longer be two, but one flesh,
and you teach us that what you have united
may never be divided.

Father, you have made the union of man and wife so holy a mystery
that it symbolizes the marriage of Christ and his Church.

Father, by your plan man and woman are united,
and married life has been established
as the one blessing that was not forfeited by original sin
or washed away in the flood.

Look with love upon this woman, your daughter,
now joined to her husband in marriage.
She asks your blessing.
Give her the grace of love and peace.
May she always follow the example of the holy women
whose praises are sung in the scriptures.

May her husband put his trust in her
and recognize that she is his equal
and the heir with him to the life of grace.
May he always honor her and love her
as Christ loves his bride, the Church.

Father, keep them always true to your commandments.
Keep them faithful in marriage
and let them be living examples of Christian life.
Give them the strength which comes from the gospel
so that they may be witnesses of Christ to others.
(Bless them with children
and help them to be good parents.
May they live to see their children's children.)
And, after a happy old age,
grant them fullness of life with the saints
    in the kingdom of heaven.

We ask this through Christ our Lord.
    R. Amen.

602

*If one or both of the parties will not be receiving Communion, the
words in brackets in the introduction are omitted.*

*If you select this option, omit the paragraph that begins "Holy
Father, you created mankind…" or the paragraph that begins "Father,
to reveal the plan of your love…," keeping the paragraph that best
corresponds to your readings.*

Phrases in parentheses are omitted should the couple be beyond childbearing years.

Let us pray to the Lord for N. and N.
who come to God's altar at the beginning of their married life
so that they may always be united in love for each other
(as now they share in the body and blood of Christ).

All pray silently for a brief moment. Then the priest continues:

Holy Father, you created mankind in your own image
and made man and woman to be joined as husband and wife
in union of body and heart
and so fulfill their mission in this world.

Father, to reveal the plan of your love,
you made the union of husband and wife
an image of the covenant between you and your people.
In the fulfillment of this sacrament,
the marriage of Christian man and woman
is a sign of the marriage between Christ and the Church.
Father, stretch out your hand, and bless N. and N.

Lord, grant that as they begin to live this sacrament
they may share with each other the gifts of your love
and become one in heart and mind
as witnesses to your presence in their marriage.
Help them to create a home together
(and give them children to be formed by the gospel
and to have a place in your family).

Give your blessings to N., your daughter,
so that she may be a good wife (and mother),
caring for the home,
faithful in love for her husband,
generous and kind.
Give your blessings to N., your son,
so that he may be a faithful husband
(and a good father).
Father, grant that as they come together to your table on earth,
so they may one day have the joy of sharing
    your feast in heaven.

We ask this through Christ our Lord.
  R. *Amen.*

603
Phrases in parentheses are omitted should the couple be beyond childbearing years.

My dear friends, let us ask God
for his continued blessings upon this bridegroom and his bride (or
N. and N.).

All pray silently for a brief moment then the priest continues:

Holy Father, creator of the universe,
maker of man and woman in your own likeness,
source of blessing for married life,
we humbly pray to you for this woman
who today is united with her husband in this sacrament of
      marriage.

May your fullest blessing come upon her and her husband
so that they may together rejoice in your gift of married love
(and enrich your Church with their children).

Lord, may they both praise you when they are happy
and turn to you in their sorrows.
May they be glad that you help them in their work
and know that you are with them in their need.
May they pray to you in the community of the Church,
and be your witnesses in the world.
May they reach old age in the company of their friends,
and come at last to the kingdom of heaven.

We ask this through Christ our Lord.
  R. *Amen.*

Prayer After Communion

  Refer to the focus of your readings, which you noted on the
appropriate work sheet. Choose a prayer after communion that
best reflects that summary. If more than one prayer fits, choose the
one you like best. Record your decision on the work sheet.

701
Lord,
in your love
you have given us this eucharist
to unite us with one another and with you.
As you have made N. and N.
one in this sacrament of marriage
(and in the sharing of the one bread and the one cup),
so now make them one in love for each other.

We ask this through Christ our Lord.

702
Lord,
we who have shared the food of your table
pray for our friends N. and N.,
whom you have joined together in marriage.
Keep them close to you always.
May their love for each other
proclaim to all the world
their faith in you.

We ask this through Christ our Lord.

703
Almighty God,
may the sacrifice we have offered
and the eucharist we have shared
strengthen the love of N. and N.,
and give us all your fatherly aid.

We ask this through Christ our Lord.

Final Blessing

Refer to the focus of your readings, which you noted on the appropriate work sheet. Choose a final blessing that best reflects that summary. If more than one blessing fits, choose the one you like best. Record your decision on the work sheet.

Phrases in parentheses are omitted for couples beyond childbearing years.

801

God the external Father keep you in love with each other,
so that the peace of Christ may stay with you
and be always in your home.
    R. *Amen.*

May (your children bless you,)
your friends console you
and all men live in peace with you.
    R. *Amen.*

May you always bear witness to the love of God in this world
so that the afflicted and the needy
will find in you generous friends,
and welcome you into the joys of heaven.
    R. *Amen.*

May almighty God bless you,
the Father, and the Son, + and the Holy Spirit.
    R. *Amen.*

802

May God, the almighty Father,
give you his joy
and bless you (in your children).
    R. *Amen.*

May the only Son of God have mercy on you
and help you in good times and in bad.
    R. *Amen.*

May the Holy Spirit of God
always fill your hearts with his love.
    R. *Amen.*
May almighty God bless you,
the Father, and the Son, + and the Holy Spirit.
    R. *Amen.*

803

May the Lord Jesus, who was a guest at the wedding in Cana,
bless you and your families and friends.
    R. *Amen.*

May Jesus, who loved his Church to the end,
always fill your hearts with his love.
   R. *Amen.*

May he grant that, as you believe in his resurrection,
so you may wait for him in joy and hope.
   R. *Amen.*

May almighty God bless you,
the Father, and the Son, + and the Holy Spirit.
   R. *Amen.*

804
May almighty God, with his Word of blessing, unite
your hearts in the never-ending bond of pure love.
   R. *Amen.*

May your children bring you happiness,
and may your generous love for them be returned to you,
many times over.
   R. *Amen.*

May the peace of Christ live always in your hearts and in
   your home.
May you have true friends to stand by you,
   both in joy and in sorrow.
May you be ready and willing to help and comfort
   all who come to you in need.
And may the blessings promised to the compassionate
   be yours in abundance.
   R. *Amen.*

May you find happiness and satisfaction in your work.
May daily problems never cause you undue anxiety,
nor the desire for earthly possessions dominate your lives.
But may your hearts' first desire be always the good things
waiting for you in the life of heaven.
   R. *Amen.*

May the Lord bless you with many happy years together,
so that you may enjoy the rewards of a good life.

And after you have served him loyally in his kingdom on earth,
may he welcome you to his eternal kingdom in heaven.
    R. *Amen.*

May almighty God bless you,
the Father, and the Son, + and the Holy Spirit.
    R. *Amen.*

General Intercessions (Prayer of the Faithful)

The prayer of the faithful takes place after the exchange of the
wedding rings. There should be four to six intercessions, presented as requests for things you and your faith community desire
from God. One petition must be for the general Church. Intercessions are NOT prayers of thanksgiving.

Several suggested intercessions are listed below. You may like
and want to use them. You may want to modify them to meet your
specific circumstances. Feel free to write your own intercessions.
This is an opportunity for you to personalize your wedding.

On a separate sheet of paper, modify these petitions or write
your own. Read aloud the intercessions you create to be sure they
sound okay. Type or write your intercessions for the person or
persons who will read them.

The presider at your wedding will introduce the intercessions
and conclude this part of the ceremony with a closing prayer of
his choosing. In weddings without a Mass, the nuptial blessing
concludes the general intercessions.

Record your intercessions on your work sheet.

For Pope N. and all Church leaders that they may lead us to
a deeper faith in God and a stronger love for one another.
We pray to the Lord.
That all civil leaders may continue to strive to base their
decisions on respect for life and the human dignity of
people. We pray to the Lord.

For God's continued blessings on N.'s and N.'s parents, who
through their shared love bestowed the gift of life and love
on them. We pray to the Lord.

That the family and friends of N. and N. may always know
God's love for them through their shared love for each other.
We pray to the Lord.

For N. and N., now united as husband and wife, that their love for each other may continue to grow and be a source of inspiration to us all. We pray to the Lord.

That our parish communities may be a place of welcome and belonging for all its members. We pray to the Lord.

For the members of this parish, that God will continue to build up their faith and they will be beacons of God's presence in the local community. We pray to the Lord.

For God's blessings on all the people that have helped N. and N. prepare for their married lives and today's celebration. We pray to the Lord.

For all couples preparing to marry and those helping them with their preparation, that they may take seriously this lifetime commitment. We pray to the Lord.

For all married couples, that they may mirror to us God's love for us and all God's people. We pray to the Lord.

For the people discerning God's call to religious life and preparing to serve our church family as priests, deacons, sisters, and brothers. We pray to the Lord.

For the single people in our church family, that together we may be a source of support and strength in the lifestyle of one another. We pray to the Lord.
For those less fortunate than ourselves: the homeless, the hungry, those struggling with relationships, the jobless, the sick and the dying. We pray to the Lord.

For all the dead, especially the deceased family members and friends of N. and N., that they may enjoy the heavenly kingdom of God. We pray to the Lord.

Rite of Marriage

Your Vows

The exchange of vows and rings takes place after the readings and homily and before the intercessions. Decide what marriage vows you want to use, how you wish to exchange vows, and what prayer for the blessing of ring(s) best fits with your readings. Record your decisions on the work sheet.

Introduction

The bride and groom stand and the minister begins:
My dear friends, you have come together in this church so that the Lord may seal and strengthen your love in the presence of the Church's minister and this community. Christ abundantly blesses this love. He has already consecrated you in baptism and now he enriches and strengthens you by a special sacrament so that you may assume the duties of marriage in mutual and lasting fidelity. And so, in the presence of the Church, I ask you to state your intentions.

Statement of Intentions

Each answers the questions separately. The third question is omitted for couples advanced in years.

Will you love and honor each other as man and wife for the rest of your lives?

N. and N., have you come here freely and without reservation to give yourselves to each other in marriage?

Will you accept children lovingly from God, and bring them up according to the law of Christ and his Church?

Exchange of Consent (Vows)

The vows may be repeated after the minister, memorized by the couple, or stated by the minister. Each of you responds "I do" if vows are stated in question form. If you wish to memorize but are fearful of going blank, you may want to type or write the vows on the back of an index or business card and put it in the palm of your free hand.
The minister begins:

Since it is your intention to enter into marriage, join your right hands, and declare your consent before God and his Church.

901

The groom says and then the bride says:
I, N., take you, N., to be my wife (husband). I promise to be true to you in good times and in bad, in sickness and in health. I will love you and honor you all the days of my life.

The same vow may be expressed in the form of a question:
N., do you take N. to be your wife (husband)? Do you promise to be true to her (him) in good times and in bad, in sickness and in health, to love her (him) and honor her (him) all the days of your life?

902

The groom says and then the bride says:
I, N., take you N., for my lawful wife (husband), to have and to hold, from this day forward, for better, for worse, for richer, for poorer, in sickness and in health, until death do us part.
The bridegroom (bride): I do.

The same vow expressed in the form of a question:
N., do you take N. for your lawful wife (husband), to have and to hold, from this day forward, for better, for worse, for richer, for poorer in sickness and in health, until death do you part?
The bridegroom (bride): I do.

Reception of Consent
Minister: You have declared your consent before the Church. May the Lord in his goodness strengthen your consent and fill you both with his blessings.
What God has joined, men must not divide.
 R. *Amen.*

Blessing of Rings
 The minister then blesses the ring(s), using one of the following blessings from which you need to choose.

1001

May the Lord bless + these rings
which you give to each other
as the sign of your love and fidelity.
    R. *Amen.*

1002

Lord, bless these rings which we bless + in your name.
Grant that those who wear them
may always have a deep faith in each other.
May they do your will
and always live together
in peace, good will, and love.
We ask this through Christ our Lord.
    R. *Amen.*

1003

Lord,
bless + and consecrate N. and N.
in their love for each other.
May these rings be a symbol
of true faith in each other,
and always remind them of their love.
We ask this through Christ our Lord.
    R. *Amen.*

Exchange of Rings

The bridegroom places the bride's ring on her hand first, saying the following (or repeating the words after the minister). Then the bride places the bridegroom's ring on his hand using the same words.

N., take this ring as a sign of my love and fidelity. In the name of the Father, and of the Son, and of the Holy Spirit.

Other Ceremonial Options

Greeting Guests

Catholics do not believe in superstitions, yet a wedding is one place superstitions have been allowed to continue. For example, one superstition is that it is bad luck for the groom to see the bride in her wedding gown prior to the procession. Let's take a look at that.

People are coming to this parish church because you invited them. It would be most impolite for you to invite people to your home and not greet them upon arrival.

Your parish is your faith home. It makes sense to welcome your guests at the church door when they arrive! Of course, that means everyone—including the groom—is going to see the bride in her gown. Some traditions and superstitions are hard to end.

Receiving your guests as they arrive at the church for the wedding celebration will do a number of things. It helps eliminate some of the tension that understandably builds up leading to the big moment. It's also a polite social use of time while everyone is waiting for the celebration to begin. More importantly, greeting your guests gives you the opportunity to thank them for coming and to invite them to participate as fully as possible in the celebration. This adds a lot of warmth that deepens participation in your ceremony. It also lessens the amount of time you will spend away from your guests for pictures. Similarly, it will eliminate the need for a receiving line after the ceremony or at the reception.

Entrance Procession

No hard-and-fast rules exist regarding the procession for the start of the celebration. There are a number of options, some more traditional than others.

The bridegroom and groomsmen, together with the clergy-man (or deacon), enter from the side of the altar or from the sacristy. Once they are in place, the bride's attendants process in from the back of church and walk down the aisle. The bride enters last in the company of her father. A variation of this is to have each groomsman walk halfway up the center aisle, offer his accompanying bridesmaid his arm, and escort her down the remainder of the aisle.

Or

The bridegroom, best man, and minister enter from the
sacristy and position themselves at the foot of the sanctuary.
The other groomsmen and bridesmaids walk down the
center aisle, hand in arm, followed by the maid of honor,
and finally the bride in the company of her father.

Or

The bride can be escorted in by both her father and mother,
since it is the love of the bride's parents for each other that
brought forth the bride's gift of life.

Or

The whole weddding party may enter in procession. The
bridegroom and bride may each be accompanied by their
parents.

Or

The whole wedding party may enter in procession, much
like Sunday Mass. The flower girl and ring bearer follow the
groomsmen and bridesmaids. The presider (bishop, priest,
or deascon) proceeds the bride and groom either escorted or
unescorted by parents, since it is the bride and groom who
administer the sacrament of matrimony to each other.

Something to think about: Why is it that the bride is "given
away" but the groom isn't? Given present-day society and the age
at which couples marry, why does anyone have to "give someone
away"?

Work with the presider officiating at your wedding and
together determine what would be most fitting for you and your
church celebration. Record whatever you decide on your "Final
Liturgy Sheet."

Music

You would never think of not having music at your reception.
Why? Because music adds a great deal to the festive nature of what
you're celebrating. For that same reason, you want music at your
wedding celebration.

Because of the sacredness of the moment, sacred music should be used at your wedding ceremony. Sacred music speaks of God's goodness, of God's love for us, and of the values we embrace as Christians. Although there are many pieces of pop music that speak of love, they are not appropriate for the sacred celebration you are planning.

Refer to the "Music Planning Guide" for a wedding ceremony with or without a Mass. For a wedding with a Mass, be sure to include the sections that are marked with an asterisk.*

Prelude music: Provide preservice music while your guests are arriving for your wedding, music that sets a mood of worship. These selections may be classical or contemporary sacred music. This music usually begins fifteen minutes prior to the celebration and may be instrumental, vocal, or a combination of both.

Entrance processional: If grandparents and parents join the congregation immediately before the ceremony begins, you may want to select something special for the moment. This could be a song or an instrumental. When the wedding party enters, you may want an additional song or instrumental. Once everyone is in place, a familiar gathering song is ideal to reflect the joy of the celebration.

Responsorial psalm: If you have a song leader, it is best to sing the responsorial psalm. In the absence of a singer, the psalm is read.

Gospel acclamation: This should be sung. If it is not possible to sing, omit it.

* *Holy Holy, memorial acclamation, amen, and communion hymn:* These are joyous moments in a Mass and should be sung. It is important that these selections are familiar to the people so they are able to participate.

Recessional: This may be an instrumental or a sung hymn.

Optional Times for Music
Unity candle ceremony: If you decide on this option, you will need a *brief* song or instrumental to accompany the action.
Presentation of gifts: This music accompanies the action taking place and should not extend beyond the action. An instrumental is appropriate and may be best.

Lamb of God: This song accompanies the breaking of bread.
Mary devotion: An appropriate song of prayer to Mary, the Mother of Jesus, can be either an instrumental or a sung hymn.

Musicians

Your musician needs a current knowledge of Church norms for music at sacred gatherings. He or she needs to be aware of the current music guidelines of your diocese and your parish. A friend or relative who is a musician or one who possesses a pleasing voice may not be the most suitable person to guide and assist you. The minister you are working with can recommend people who possess the necessary knowledge and experience you need.

Readers

Choose persons who have been trained to proclaim the Word of God in their church. They will read the first reading (and the second reading) and the responsorial psalm if it is not sung. The priest or deacon proclaims the gospel. If you have chosen two readings along with the gospel, consider asking a married couple to read, since this is a celebration of the union of a man and a woman in the sacrament of matrimony. Your readers may be family members, godparents, newly married close friends, or perhaps a couple involved in your preparation program.

Also choose a person or couple to read the general intercessions.

If you have trouble securing capable and willing people to read, the minister working with you can recommend good readers from your faith community.

Wedding Party Arrangement at the Exchange of Vows

After the homily, vows and weddings rings are exchanged. Where you, the minister, and your wedding party stand during this time depends on the configuration of the sanctuary. Many brides and grooms stand facing the minister, with their backs to the assembly. So invited guests can participate more fully and can clearly view the ceremony, it is recommended that the two of you, along with your best man and maid of honor (and perhaps the rest of your wedding party) stand at the front of the sanctuary facing the community. The minister then stands either off to the side between the wedding party and the congregation or down the center aisle amid the assembly. Before finalizing your plans, discuss all your options with the person officiating at your wedding.

Unity Candle

The lighting of the unity candle is not an official part of the Rite of Marriage. Bishops, priests, and liturgists question this practice because, among other reasons, there is no clear understanding of the gesture. Many interpretations are given the movement. It appears as a duplication of what has already been said and symbolized by the exchange of wedding vows and rings.

There are instances in which couples use their baptismal candles at the side of the unity candle. After lighting the unity candle, instead of extinguishing the two side candles, the baptismal candle remain aflame as a sign of the continuation of their baptismal commitment being lived out now in the sacrament of matrimony. What does the extinguishing of the side candles mean? Do the two people lose or must give up their individuality? See the confusion the action may cause in understanding the gesture?

It would be best to discuss the idea of a unity candle and its meaning with the minister officiating at your wedding.

Gifts and Gift Presenters

Bread and wine are the primary gifts offered during Mass. As a visible sign of your intentions to be Christlike to others, especially the poor and less fortunate, you may include nonperishable foods or a financial contribution to a charitable organization together with the gifts of bread and wine.

Gift presenters should be Catholics who have received the sacrament of Eucharist. Godparents, family members, or good friends can present the gifts. Gifts are presented after the prayers of the faithful.

Eucharistic Ministers

You may need additional ministers for Communion to assist the priest. Are either of you, your parents, or other family members eucharistic ministers? Do you know someone in the parish who is a eucharistic minister? If you have trouble securing capable and willing people to be eucharistic ministers, the minister working with you can recommend parishioners.

Receiving Line

A receiving line is your opportunity to personally thank your guests for coming. Ideally, you greet your guests as they arrive; there are other options, however. You can form a line, with your parents and wedding party, in the vestibule or outside the church doors following the ceremony. You can form this same kind of line at your reception or you can personally thank each guest as you mingle at the reception.

For a number of reasons, many parishes do not allow a receiving line at the church. Check with your minister to learn what is and is not acceptable.

Reception

Your reception celebration should be joyful and conducted with dignity, keeping in mind the sacredness of the sacrament just received. At some receptions, the garter worn by the bride is removed by the groom to the music of "The Stripper." This garter is then thrown by the groom into a group of single men and the bride throws her bouquet into a group of single women. Those who catch these items are deemed "the next to be married." A photographer may ask them to pose for a picture in which the man slides the garter onto the lady's leg. Usually, this scene is accompanied by the jeering encouragement of onlookers.

How does this behavior reflect the gospel values professed at the wedding service? Do you want to put any of your guests in an embarrassing situation? Does the behavior and response evoked from your guests reflect your values for respect of the whole person and mature adult sexuality? Do some "traditions" need to be changed?

Further Celebration Considerations

Photographs and Video Taping

Many parishes have regulations concerning pictures. You and your photographer and video person need to know these regulations prior to making decisions about pictures. These regulations concern the time available for pictures before and after the wedding, the use of flash, the placement of the video cameras, and the movement of the photographer and video person during the wedding. You do not want to turn the church into a studio. Ask the minister or parish staff person working with you about regulations.

If you plan to use the church for pictures, loud conversation, smoking, and drinking are not appropriate behaviors in the presence of Christ reserved in the tabernacle.

Runners, Candles, and Flowers

Your parish may have regulations concerning flowers, candles, and runners, as well as throwing rice, confetti, flower petals, bird seed, and the like. Check with the parish before contacting a florist or making any definite plans.

Runners: In the past, the runner was used to keep the hem of the wedding gown clean. Today, the runner is another ornamentational expense. It slips, and people slip on it. If you have a runner, make sure it is secure and does not become a hazard.

Candles: Many parishes prohibit hurricane candles or other types of candles along the church aisle. Likewise, there may be regulations about the use of candles in the sanctuary. Check with the parish about candle regulations before making any decisions.

Flowers: Flowers in the sanctuary should be live and authentic rather than artificial, symbolizing the reality of your love and commitment. Flowers are not required, but welcomed. They should be arranged simply, leaving the altar unobstructed. Likewise, flowers should not block the view of the lectern top.

Keep in mind the liturgical season of your wedding. During the Christmas season, there may be poinsettias in the sanctuary; lilies or other colorful flower arrangements may be in the sanctuary during the Easter season. The absence of flowers in the sanctuary during the Lenten season is proper.

Wedding Booklet

A worship aid booklet is nice to have and can be a keepsake of your special day. These are especially nice for guests who are not familiar with the people involved in the ceremony, the music, and the prayers in which they are expected to participate. On the other hand, booklets are one more expense and not necessary.

Copyright permission must be granted for lyrics and for music printed in a booklet. Ask your parish if they have the copyrights to the music and the lyrics you want to duplicate.

In lieu of creating your own original booklet cover, preprinted covers can be purchased from Christian bookstores, catalogs, and supply houses.

Your musician or officiating minister should be able to assist you with booklet covers and content.

Flowers to Mary

This devotion consists of taking flowers to a statue or picture of Mary, the Mother of Jesus. The two of you silently ask Mary to remain a close friend and role model to you throughout your marriage.

In some parishes, statues or shrines to Mary are at the far side of the church or in the back. In this case, you could invite your guests to join you in prayer to Mary. If you have a wedding booklet, you might include the Hail Mary or the Memorare for all to pray together with you instead of taking flowers.

While honoring Mary in some fashion during the wedding ceremony or Mass has been a custom in some places by some people, the practice is not part of the Rite of Marriage and is not required.

Rehearsal

The purpose of the rehearsal is to familiarize and put at ease those you have invited to participate in your wedding ceremony in an attempt to make everything move along nicely. Who should be at the rehearsal?

- Parents and perhaps grandparents
- Members of your wedding party, including all ushers, flower girls, ring bearers, junior bridesmaids, and groomsmen
- Scripture readers and the person(s) doing the prayer of the faithful
- Officiating minister and servers, especially if they are unfamiliar with the church
- Gift presenters, candlelighters, and eucharistic ministers

It is best if the musicians rehearse at another time. Consult your minister or parish staff person to arrange a time for the music rehearsal.

With all the consulting and planning you have done in preparation for your wedding ceremony, be sensitive yet firm when family and friends make suggestions at the rehearsal. Stick to your plans. Your decisiveness will keep the rehearsal moving and will help keep you and others from becoming upset.

Fees

Use of church: Fees vary from diocese to diocese and parish to parish. If your parish has no set fee, your contribution should take into consideration the amount of time church personnel have invested in your preparation and wedding ceremony plans. Compare what you might contribute with what you are paying for dresses, flowers, photographers, caterers, use of the hall, music, invitations, and other amenities.

Minister: It is proper to give a monetary gift to the officiating minister, beyond your contribution for the use of the church.

Servers: It is proper to give a monetary gift to servers. These gifts are usually presented by the best man on behalf of the bride and groom prior to the ceremony.

Musicians, florist, photographer, and others you hire to perform a service at your wedding and throughout the day will let you know their standard fees.

Closing Comments

A Day of Joy

There are many ways to make your wedding day special. We have shared just some ideas of how you can enhance the celebration. There are more, such as the ethnic customs brought to our U.S. Church by people of different nationalities. If a cultural tradition is a part of your ethnic heritage, your family should be helpful in assisting you with these preparations. Be sure to explain these customs to the priest or deacon officiating at your wedding so he understands what you wish to do and why. Finalize all wedding ceremony plans with the clergyman presiding at your wedding.

It is our hope that we have been able to help you prepare your ceremony. Together, we are the Church, the people of God. You are an important part of our faith community. Your wedding day is a special day. It should reflect the faith we profess and the commitment we live within the faith community.

Your celebration has to mean more than a good time. Your wedding day "I do" is meant for your happiness and fulfillment, through the graces of God, as well as for the good and joy of the whole Christian community. Anyone can marry, but in the Catholic Church we receive the sacrament of matrimony..

Kathleen McAnany
Peter Schavitz, C.SS.R.

NOTES